LAKE FOREST LIBRARY
360 E. Deerpath
Lake Forest, IL 60045
(847) 234-0648

Seeds of a Nation

Connecticut

Sheila Wyborny

KIDHAVEN
PRESS™

THOMSON
———✦———™
GALE

San Diego • Detroit • New York • San Francisco • Cleveland
New Haven, Conn. • Waterville, Maine • London • Munich

© 2003 by KidHaven Press. KidHaven Press is an imprint of The Gale Group, Inc., a division of Thomson Learning, Inc.

KidHaven™ and Thomson Learning™ are trademarks used herein under license.

For more information, contact
KidHaven Press
27500 Drake Rd.
Farmington Hills, MI 48331-3535
Or you can visit our Internet site at http://www.gale.com

LIBRARY OF CONGRESS CATALOGING-IN-PUBLICATION DATA

Wyborny, Sheila, 1950–
    Connecticut / by Sheila Wyborny.
        p. cm. — (Seeds of a nation)
Summary: Discusses the early history of Connecticut beginning with the Native Americans who have lived there for many years, through European exploration and settlement, to statehood in 1788.
Includes bibliographical references (p.) and index.
    ISBN 0-7377-1445-X (alk. paper)
        1. Connecticut—History—Colonial period, ca. 1600–1775—Juvenile literature.
2. Connecticut–History—1775–1865—Juvenile literature. [1. Connecticut—History—Colonial period, ca. 1600—1775. 2. Connecticut—History—1775–1865.] I. Title. II. Series.
    F94.3.W93 2003
    974.6'02--dc21
                                                    2002155894

Printed in the United States of America

Contents

Chapter One
The Land and Its First People 4

Chapter Two
Newcomers 13

Chapter Three
From Conflict to Colony 21

Chapter Four
Wars, Revolution, and Statehood 28

Facts About Connecticut 38

Places to Visit in Connecticut 40

Glossary 41

For Further Exploration 43

Index 44

Picture Credits 47

About the Author 48

Chapter One

The Land and Its First People

Connecticut is in the northeastern United States. It shares its northern border with Massachusetts, to the east is Rhode Island, its western neighbor is New York, and to the south is Long Island Sound, a waterway off the Atlantic Ocean.

Connecticut has five land regions. The western third of the state is called the Western New England Upland. It is hilly with many rivers. A twenty-mile strip through the central part of the state is known as the Connecticut Valley Lowland. It has low hills and rich soil good for growing fruits and vegetables. It is also a region of dairy farms.

Eastern Connecticut is part of the Eastern New England Upland. This region also has rich soil. Corn, potatoes, and wheat are grown in this area, and it is also home to many poultry farms.

The Coastal Lowlands is a narrow belt along the shoreline of Long Island Sound. This is the center of the state's industry and also much of its population.

Finally, the Taconic Section is the northwest corner of the state. This area is the site of the state's highest elevation of only twenty-six hundred feet.

These drastically different regions were formed many thousands of years ago.

From the Ice Age

Fourteen thousand years ago, the region we know as New England was just emerging from the **Ice Age**, a

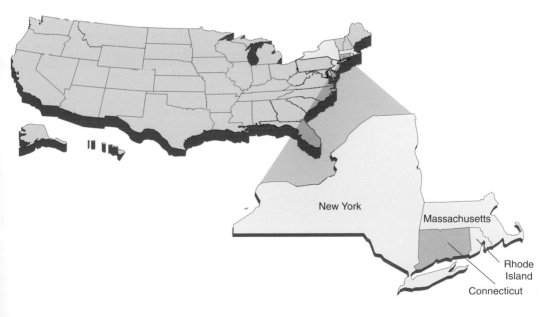

Connecticut's Place in the United States Today

New York

Massachusetts

Rhode Island

Connecticut

time when huge glaciers, massive sheets of ice miles wide and weighing many tons, began receding from North America, carving valleys into the earth. Slowly, the plant life of the forests and meadows grew.

A few thousand years after the glaciers receded but while the climate was still cold, herds of large cold-tolerant animals, **mastodons** and **woolly mammoths**, migrated into this area. These herds were followed by hunters.

After the large woolly mammoths and mastodons disappeared, Paleo-Indians hunted caribou (pictured), elk, and deer for meat.

Arrival of the First People

With the retreat of the glaciers and the arrival of the large animals, the first people came into this woodland region. They are known as the **Paleo-Indians**. The Paleo-Indians were hunters and gatherers. This means that they survived by hunting animals for meat and by finding edible plants. Some of the plants they found were wild strawberries, apples, mushrooms, nuts, and wild rice. They also caught fish in the streams and rivers.

But as the climate continued to warm, the large animals, which were originally from a very cold climate far to the northwest, began to die. To survive, the Paleo-Indians began hunting smaller animals, like deer and elk.

With abundant game, fish, and wild fruits and vegetables, the Paleo-Indians remained in the northeastern corner of what is now the United States, and as time passed, they developed into cultural groups.

Native Americans of the Forests

From these first people descended several groups, all known as part of the Algonquian language group.

The four main groups were the Matabesec, who lived in the hills of western Connecticut; the Sequin, who settled along the Connecticut River; the Nipmuc, the peaceful people of the northeast forests; and the Pequot, who inhabited the southeastern forests. Of these groups, the Pequot (whose name means "destroyers of men") fought for control of the area and were usually victorious in battle. Later, a group split from

Discovered in Connecticut, Pequot petroglyphs provide clues about the tribe's history, lifestyle, and beliefs.

the Pequot and called themselves the Mohegan. They were also fierce fighters.

Although these groups settled in different parts of the area now known as Connecticut and fought over hunting territory, their lives were similar.

Living from the Land

For these people of the forests, nature was their super-market. From their environment they could find everything they needed.

From trees they built the framework for their homes and made some of their canoes, called dugouts. The trees provided material from which these early people made musical instruments and containers. They also tapped the sap from maple trees. From the sap of these trees they could make sweet syrup and sugar. Bark from birch trees served as skin for another type of canoe called a birchbark. Because of the light-colored bark of the tree, these canoes looked almost white.

Plants provided food and medicines. They also provided weaving materials and dyes.

Animals gave the Native Americans of the forests meat for food and skins for warmth. And since these people wasted nothing, they used the bones and teeth of some of the animals for making tools and decorations.

Nor did the Native Americans overlook the waterways. They harvested the rivers and bays for fish and shellfish. Shells became tools and decorative items. Parts of some shells were also used as **wampum**, their form of money.

These tribes developed complex societies, with different roles and responsibilities for the members of their villages.

Life in the Village and the Beginnings of Trade

To the outsider, it might have appeared that the women did all of the work in the village, and they did have many responsibilities. The Native Americans of the northeast had developed farming techniques. The planting and harvesting of the crops was the responsibility of the women. In addition to farming, women took care of the children, tended the fires, and cooked the food. Since nothing went to waste, the women also cleaned and tanned the skins of the animals the villagers ate. The skins were used for blankets and to cover their round, dome-shaped, single-room dwellings called **wigwams**.

When the game supply dwindled and the village had to be moved to an area with more plentiful game, the women also had to pack all of the belongings of their families. They removed the coverings from the wigwams and packed them as well, and hauled their

Wigwams like this one were constructed from nearby trees and covered with bark and animal skins for protection.

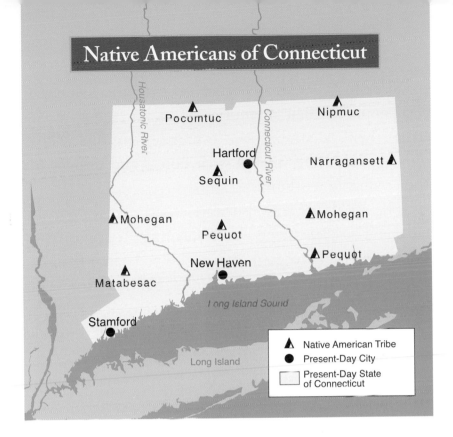

Native Americans of Connecticut

Housatonic River

Pocomtuc

Nipmuc

Hartford

Connecticut River

Sequin

Narragansett

Mohegan

Pequot

Mohegan

New Haven

Pequot

Matabesac

Long Island Sound

Stamford

▲ Native American Tribe
● Present-Day City
☐ Present-Day State of Connecticut

Long Island

packed belongings to the site where the new village would be built.

The men also had plenty of work to keep them busy. When the families arrived at the site selected for the new village, the men cleared the land. Then they cut saplings to make the framework for new wigwams. As the women worked to get the new village in order, the men hunted for game. The men also made the canoes that were used to transport some of their belongings down the river to their new village site.

Additionally, the men had the responsibility of defending the village from all invaders, animals or men.

Older people, those who were no longer able to fish, farm, or hunt, also had duties in the village. It was their job to make the nets for fishing, carve tools, and make pots. The older people also held the history of the people in their memories and told stories of the tribe's history around the evening campfire. These older people were treated with honor and respect for their valuable wisdom.

The children were also important members of the village. The girls helped with farming. Younger boys, those too young to go on hunts, helped catch fish.

Even their play prepared the children for their future roles. Girls learned to take care of babies by tending their cornhusk dolls. Boys learned hunting skills by practicing with toy bows and arrows.

The cultures of all of the northeastern Native American groups were orderly and in harmony with nature. In the 1600s, however, that harmony would be interrupted and the lives of the woodland people would never be the same.

Change began with the arrival of the first Europeans. By the time the Europeans arrived, six or seven thousand Indians lived in what is now Connecticut. The Europeans were interested in exploiting this new land, and one of their first efforts was to begin trading with the Indians. The Europeans traded blankets, iron tools, cloth, glass beads, and firearms. The Indians traded furs. These furs sold in Europe for a great deal of money. And as word spread of the riches of the region, more Europeans arrived on the shores of North America and journeyed inland.

Chapter Two

Newcomers

Europe had long heard rumors of a wild and rich land far across the ocean to the west. A number of countries in Europe believed the rumors and financed voyages to this strange land. Most of the explorers came for the same reason. The explorers were to claim the New World for their home countries and exploit the new area's wealth. This led to conflict because the government of one country might ignore another country's claim that its explorers had arrived first and that they controlled the land and its resources. This happened in the land that became the Connecticut colony when the Dutch and the English both wanted to control this region.

The Dutch

Dutch explorer Adriaen Block, the first known European to explore Connecticut, arrived in the area almost by accident. He had crossed the Atlantic in his ship, the *Tiger*, in 1613, but the ship was destroyed by fire.

With the help of friendly Indians on Manhattan Island, Block and his crew built another ship and called it the *Onrust*, the Dutch word for restless. The ship was too small to cross the Atlantic and return to the Netherlands, so Block and his crew explored inland. With this smaller ship, Block was able to navigate the Connecticut coast and travel up the Connecticut River in 1614. Block wanted to set up trade between the Dutch and the Indians. He claimed the

Dutch explorer Adriaen Block and his crew hack lumber for their ship, the Onrust.

region for the Netherlands. Retracing his journey to the coast, Block and his crew encountered a larger ship and were finally able to return home to the Netherlands with stories of a beautiful and rich land. Block's stories drew the attention of other people from the Netherlands. One of these people was Jacob van Curler, who traveled there in 1633.

Although Block had already claimed this land for the Netherlands, Jacob van Curler purchased a tract of this land from the Indians. Financed by the Dutch West India Company, a trading and colonizing company, van Curler made plans to set up trade with the Indians. Van Curler wanted a good relationship with the Indians, and he felt that formally paying for the land would show the Indians his good intentions. Here, he established his fort and trading post, which he named House of Hope. Today, this area is called Dutch Point, near present-day Hartford. With the success of van Curler's trading post, more Dutch settlers came into the area, bought land from the Indians, and began trading with them.

During these early years, the Dutch enjoyed a peaceful and profitable relationship with the Indians, but this peaceful time would be limited.

The English

Although the Dutch were already in Connecticut and had a trade relationship with the Indians by the time the English arrived, the English felt they were entitled to explore and develop the region as well. In 1632

Edward Winslow sailed from the Plymouth Colony in 1632 to establish the earliest English settlement in Connecticut.

Pilgrim Edward Winslow came from the Plymouth Colony, sailing up the Connecticut River as far as present-day Windsor. There, he bought some land from the Indians to establish his settlement. Winslow would not be the only Englishman to lay claim to land in Connecticut.

In 1633 English colonists William Holmes and John Oldham also sailed up the Connecticut River, each bringing groups of people with the intention of establishing settlements. After a skirmish with the Dutch, Holmes and his men built a log house and surrounded it with a palisade (stockade) to protect it from the Indians and the Dutch. A month later, seventy Dutch soldiers arrived, intending to drive out Holmes and his settlers, but they refused to leave. The Dutch commander decided that the settlement was not important enough to fight over, so the English remained. This was the beginning of English control of Connecticut. Oldham and his followers established the community of Wethersfield. But Oldham did not have long to live in his new community. A few years later, he was killed by Indians.

Several communities were founded between 1633 and 1635, but a harsh winter in 1635 drove away many of the colonists. They returned in the spring, though,

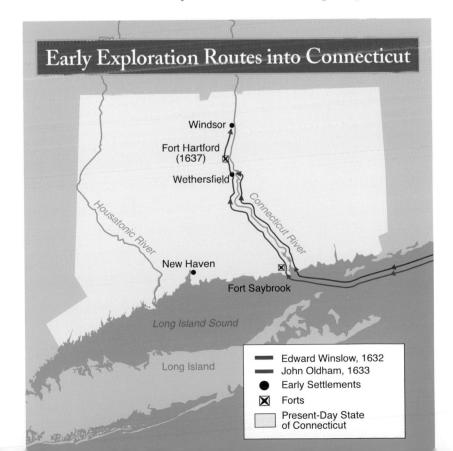

Early Exploration Routes into Connecticut

Windsor

Fort Hartford (1637)

Wethersfield

Housatonic River

Connecticut River

New Haven

Fort Saybrook

Long Island Sound

Long Island

— Edward Winslow, 1632
— John Oldham, 1633
● Early Settlements
☒ Forts
☐ Present-Day State of Connecticut

Puritan reverend Thomas Hooker leads a group of Puritans into Hartford.

bringing many more settlers with them. Some of the new settlers who came to Connecticut and built communities during this time came for reasons other than the rich resources.

The Puritans

Some settlers came to Connecticut for freedom of religion. In 1636 the Puritans founded Hartford, Connecticut, which is today Connecticut's capital city, and later founded New Haven, near Long Island Sound. The Puritans felt that the Massachusetts Bay Colony was becoming too crowded and they wanted a place where they would be left alone to worship their own way in peace. This group of Puritans was led by Reverend Thomas Hooker.

The Puritans had a positive effect on the developing government of Connecticut. Hooker and his followers believed strongly in education. They believed that all people should be able to read the Bible. In fact, as soon as Connecticut was settled, a law was passed requiring all settlements to provide schools. With the building of schools, the settlements were more like real towns, places where children as well as adults had their own roles in the family and the community.

Daily Life of Settlers

Most of the Connecticut settlers earned their living as farmers. The rich soil in the river valleys grew more food than they could use, and so they sold the surplus vegetables to settlers in the other colonies. The work

A group of colonial emigrants treks through the snow to reach the fertile soil of the Connecticut Valley in time for the next season's plantings.

was difficult, keeping them busy from daylight until dark. In addition to tending crops, the settlers also had to build their own homes. When new settlers arrived, the townspeople would gather to help them build their cabins. In addition to building their homes, they had to make their own furniture as well.

As soon as sons were old enough and large enough to help, they worked in the fields alongside their parents and helped build cabins for new families. The men and boys also hunted and fished.

The girls helped at home, spinning yarn, weaving cloth, and making clothing and candles. They also helped cook and clean. This included tending the fireplace, where the cooking was done. As soon as a school was established in the community, the children had to do their chores before and after school.

Life in the settlement was not only hard work—at times it was also very dangerous.

Chapter Three

From Conflict to Colony

When the Dutch and English first arrived, the Indians were friendly and helpful. Not only did they trade with the Europeans, they also shared their own food with them. But the Indians did not understand what it meant when the Europeans purchased land from them. The Indians thought that the Europeans would stay for a while, hunt and fish, and then move on the same way the Indians did. To the Indians of the northeast, land could be used by everyone; no one owned it. They thought that they could continue to hunt and fish the land as they had for generations. However, when the Dutch and later the English bought parcels of land from the Indians, they expected the Indians to leave the land for good. This misunderstanding, and acts of violence on the parts of both Indians and Europeans, led to a very violent period in Connecticut's history.

A Pequot Indian presents an arrow as a declaration of war against the colonists in a Connecticut settlement.

Beginnings of Conflict

The Pequot, a group of Indians who lived in the area of present-day southern Connecticut, was the largest Indian group in the region. Their tribe was equal to all to the other Connecticut tribes put together. Although they had been helpful to the Europeans, the Pequot could also be fierce warriors. They were upset by the arrival of Europeans into the lands they had always inhabited and hunted. When an unidentified white man killed one of their **sachems**, or leaders, they were enraged. At first their attacks were isolated. In 1634 they killed Captain John Stone, an English trader. The Pequot said that Stone mistreated them.

When Indians murdered Captain John Oldham, who had helped found Wethersfield, the Pequot protected the killers, who were not members of their tribe, and refused to turn them over to the English. In revenge, the English, joined by Mohegan allies, killed several Pequot and destroyed their homes. This was the beginning of one of the most tragic periods in the history of the thirteen colonies.

Bloody Times

Enraged by the attack on one of their villages, the Pequot attacked Wethersfield and several other Connecticut settlements between the winter of 1636 and the spring of 1637. The Pequot were reported to have killed around two dozen colonists during this time.

In May 1637 the colonists held an emergency meeting in Hartford and formed a **militia** to stop the Pequot. They knew that if they did not defeat the Pequot, not only Connecticut but surrounding colonies would be in danger of attack. Captain John Mason was placed in charge of an army of one hundred settlers from Connecticut and Massachusetts and several hundred Indian allies, mostly Narragansett and Mohegan. Since the Mohegan had once been part of the Pequot, their knowledge of Pequot habits would be valuable in battle. In June of the same year, Mason and his troops destroyed a large Pequot village near the location of present-day West Mystic, Connecticut. Nearly seven hundred Pequot Indians died in this raid. Some of the Pequot escaped into a swampland near Fairfield, Connecticut, but they were hunted down also. The few survivors were divided up to be slaves of the English and of their Indian allies. Although the colonial soldiers felt they were avenging the murdered colonists, this attack resulted in the terrible slaughter of defenseless people.

Captain John Mason's militia rests at Porter's Rocks, Connecticut, the night before attacking a Pequot village.

Colonial settlers and Indian allies virtually wiped out the entire Pequot tribe.

Colonial troops continued to rout the Pequot until nearly all were either killed or sold into slavery. The total destruction of the Pequot tribe was a terrible shock to the other Indians in Connecticut, even those who were English allies, and convinced other tribes in the region who might have opposed the English that they, too, would be destroyed. Once Indian resistance was taken care of, more settlers streamed into the region.

Soldiers returning to Massachusetts after the Pequot War told their friends and neighbors about the beautiful land and plentiful resources in Connecticut and soon more settlers came to the region. And as the Connecticut colony grew, a system of government was needed to provide laws and protect the rights of the colonists.

A System of Government

In the spring of 1638, Reverend Thomas Hooker, a founder of Hartford, Connecticut, preached a sermon. It was to become the basis of government for the Connecticut colony. In his sermon he said, "The foundation of authority is laid, firstly, in the free consent of the people."

Reverend Thomas Hooker preaches in 1638. The words of his sermon served to define Connecticut's governmental powers and procedures.

This means that the citizens should have a say in how they are governed. Hooker believed that the people should choose their own officials, but the people should also be very careful when making this selection. He said that the powers of elected officials should be limited, giving no official the opportunity for total control. He felt that people would be much more likely to go along with the decisions of their leaders if they, the people, had chosen their leaders.

This sermon became the Fundamental Orders of 1639. This was the system of government adopted by Connecticut. There were five basic ideas expressed in the system of orders. The people would elect their officials. There would be no taxation without representation. The number of elected officials would be in proportion with the number of people in the community. All **freedmen**, former slaves who had taken an oath to be faithful to the government, could vote. And any new towns settled in Connecticut would be under the same form of government.

The Fundamental Orders of 1639 has been called the first written constitution in the English-speaking world. It was adopted as a system of government for other colonies and later served as one of the models for the United States Constitution. But even though Connecticut had developed a generally fair and impartial system of government and settlers continued arriving in droves, more turmoil lay ahead.

Chapter Four

Wars, Revolution, and Statehood

The outcome of the Pequot War broke the spirit of many of the Indians, and peace reigned for about thirty-six years as the Indians and the settlers maintained an uneasy **truce**. But as years passed, the Indians' resentment of the settlers resurfaced. A war waged by one Indian sachem would begin a hundred years of war for the colonists. Before this violent century ended, the colonists would fight the Indians, the French, and, in order to free themselves from what they felt was British tyranny, the colonists would also be at war with the English.

King Philip's War
Wampanoag sachem Metacomet (called King Philip by the colonists because he was so vain and superior)

was very angry with the New England colonists. Despite the fact that his father, Massasoit, had befriended the Pilgrims when they arrived in the New World in 1620, over the years the New England colonists had mistreated the Indians in many ways. They ran the Indians off of their own land and tried to force them to become Christians, sometimes physically abusing the Indians. The colonists may even have murdered Metacomet's brother.

Wampanoag Indian leader Metacomet, also known as King Philip, led hundreds of Indians in an effort to force colonists from Connecticut.

In 1675 Metacomet organized the Wampanoag, the Narragansett, who were angry with the colonists, and several other tribes in an effort to drive the colonists out of their settlements. This period of battles from 1675 to 1676 was called King Philip's War. The only town Metacomet attacked in Connecticut was Simsbury. Connecticut's colonial government sent several hundred colonists to assist New England's army of one thousand soldiers in fighting Metacomet and his followers.

In December 1675 the New England army attacked a large Indian village, where about three thousand people were spending the winter. The colonial soldiers

Settlers killed Metacomet in 1676, ending King Philip's War after more than a year of bloody fighting.

set the village ablaze. Many children as well as adults burned to death and many more were shot as they ran from the burning village. Although the Indians fought back and killed or wounded several hundred soldiers, by the time the battle ended, a third of the villagers lay dead.

Several months later Metacomet's own family was captured and sold into slavery. Finally, on August 12, 1676, Metacomet was tracked down and killed, bringing the war to an end. But peace did not last for long.

French and Indian Conflict on American Soil

Fourteen years after the end of King Philip's War, France and England began fighting for control of North America. Since most of the Indians felt that they were treated better by the French than by the English, and in fact many French traders and trappers had married Indian women, many of the Indians chose to fight with the French against the English. This period of time from 1689 to 1763 was called the Colonial Wars or the French and Indian Wars.

There were actually four separate wars fought during these years: King William's War (1689–1697), Queen Anne's War (1702–1713), King George's War (1744–1748), and the French and Indian War (1754–1763).

Although none of the battles of these wars was fought in Connecticut, Connecticut sent hundreds of soldiers to help its neighboring colonies over the years, and many of these soldiers were killed in battle. Once again, there would be only a few brief years of peace before the Connecticut colonists were involved in yet another war.

The War for Independence

In the last quarter of the 1700s, the British government wanted to strengthen its control over Connecticut and the other colonies in North America and to gain as much wealth from them as possible. Great Britain placed heavy taxes on such items as sugar and tea. The British also imposed the **Stamp Act**, a tax that made the colonists pay for special stamps on all printed documents. The colonists were outraged. They felt all of these taxes were terribly unfair and they did not think they should be ruled by a country that was so far away.

Soon the colonies were embroiled in a full-blown revolution. The Connecticut colony had begun training their militia in October 1774. They provided food, guns, and ammunition for their soldiers and soldiers from other colonies. In June 1775 over two hundred Connecticut soldiers joined soldiers from the other colonies in the Battle of Bunker Hill in Massachusetts. Although this battle was a victory for the British, one thousand of their soldiers were killed or wounded. The colonial troops had only four hundred killed or wounded.

But this was not the only time Connecticut soldiers defended American soil outside of their own colony. They also fought in the Battles of Long Island, New York, and Trenton, New Jersey, both in 1776, and in the Battles of Saratoga, New York, and Germantown, Pennsylvania, both in 1777.

Colonists protest the Stamp Act by burning the special British stamps.

No famous Revolutionary War battles were fought in Connecticut, but the colony was raided by the British several times. The British attacked Danbury in April 1777 and Greenwich in 1779, but were run out by the Connecticut militia. They also attacked New Haven and Fairfield in 1779, destroying hundreds of buildings and killing several townspeople, and finally they destroyed Norwalk, Connecticut.

On July 4, 1776, delegates from all thirteen of the colonies signed the Declaration of Independence, declaring themselves free of British rule. Not long after the signing, a young Connecticut soldier made history and lost his life.

Nathan Hale and Benedict Arnold

Connecticut native Nathan Hale had been a school-teacher, but he wanted to help fight for the freedom of the colonies, so in 1775 he joined the Continental Army. By September 1776 Hale was made a captain and put in command of nearly two hundred soldiers. That same month, Hale volunteered to go on a spying mission, knowing that capture would mean death. He was successful for several days, but was captured before he could return to his own troops. He was convicted of spying and was sentenced to hang the next day. Before the sentence was carried out, he was asked if he had any final words. Hale answered, "I only regret that I have but one life to lose for my country."

On September 22, 1776, twenty-one-year-old Hale was hanged, but his words remain one of the most famous quotations of the Revolutionary War. Hale was an American hero, but another Connecticut citizen earned a reputation as a traitor.

Benedict Arnold was from Norwich, Connecticut. Early in the Revolutionary War, Arnold had earned the rank of general and became a hero when he helped capture cannons from the British fort Ticonderoga. He also fought courageously at Quebec and at Lake Champlain. But other officers were promoted over Arnold, making him very angry. In 1780 while in

American patriot Nathan Hale is prepared for hanging as his British captors look on.

command of West Point, New York, Arnold made plans to turn the fort over to the British, but his plans were discovered. Arnold escaped capture and later fought with the British against the colonists in Virginia and in his own home colony. He left America for Great Britain and died there in 1801. Throughout the rest of his life and even today, the name Benedict Arnold is synonymous with traitor.

Despite Arnold's betrayal of his country, the Revolutionary War and the fighting came to an end in 1783. The colonies won the war and began a new country.

And Finally Statehood

Connecticut became the fifth state in the new United States on January 9, 1788. Some of the early settlers who had worked so hard to clear their land and fought to keep it became major landowners. Others brought their own special skills to Connecticut.

By the 1800s some Connecticut citizens were inventing useful devices. In 1792 Eli Whitney invented the cotton gin and in 1835 Samuel Colt patented a pistol that bears his name. In 1843 Charles Thurber invented the typewriter.

Also during this time, Connecticut began developing into a leader in manufacturing and remains a manufacturing center today. But part of Connecticut's economy also comes from insurance, banking, health care, and tourism.

Many of Connecticut's small settlements, like New Haven, prospered after Connecticut became the fifth state in the new United States.

Eli Whitney developed the cotton gin in his Connecticut workshop. Whitney's invention revolutionized the way cotton was harvested.

Connecticut is also home to many fine universities, such as Yale University in New Haven and, despite its small size, Connecticut has over forty public and private universities.

Connecticut is a good place to spend a vacation or a lifetime.

Facts About Connecticut

State motto: *Quit Transtulit Sustinet* (He Who Is Transplanted Still Sustains)

State nickname: Constitution State, Nutmeg State

State song: "Yankee Doodle"

State capital: Hartford

State flower: mountain laurel

State bird: robin

State tree: white oak

State mineral: garnet

State animal: sperm whale

State shellfish: eastern oyster

State insect: European mantis

Famous people: Ethan Allen, P.T. Barnum, Samuel Colt, Charles Goodyear, Katharine Hepburn, Ralph Nader, Paul Newman, Eugene O'Neill, Harriet Beecher Stowe, Mark Twain, Noah Webster, Eli Whitney

Agriculture: apples, greenhouse and nursery products, milk, chickens, eggs

Manufacturing: transportation equipment, food products, chemicals, machinery, fabricated metal products,
electrical equipment, scientific instruments

Mining: crushed stone, sand

Places to Visit in Connecticut

Bridgeport: Beardsley Zoo, Discovery Museum

Bristol: American Clock and Watch Museum, Lake Compounce Theme Park

Coventry: The Nathan Hale Homestead

East Haddam: Gillette Castle

Groton: USS Nautilus and Submarine Force Museum

Hamden: The Eli Whitney Museum

Hartford: The Harriet Beecher Stowe Center, The Mark Twain House, The Old State House

Mashantucket: Mashantucket Pequot Museum and Research Center

Mystic: Mystic Aquarium and Institute for Exploration, Mystic Seaport

New Britain: New Britain Museum of American Art, New Britain Industrial Museum

New Haven: Peabody Museum of Natural History, Yale University Art Gallery, Yale Center for British Art

Niantic: The Children's Museum

Norwalk: The Maritime Aquarium, Sheffield Island Lighthouse

Rocky Hill: Dinosaur State Park

Glossary

freedman: A former slave.

Ice Age: A time when huge sheets of ice covered much of Europe, North and South America, and parts of Asia.

mastodon: A huge, prehistoric mammal from which elephants are believed to have descended.

militia: A military unit whose members work other jobs when not in service.

Paleo-Indians: Earliest Native Americans who followed prehistoric herds into North America from Asia.

sachem: A high official or chief of a Native American tribe.

Stamp Act: A law passed by British Parliament in 1765 that required colonists to purchase stamps for all paper goods issued in the colonies.

truce: A temporary interruption of war or fighting.

wampum: Beads made from polished shells used by some Native American groups as money.

wigwam: A dome-shaped home of Native Americans of the northeast, made of a pole framework overlaid with tree bark or animal hides.

woolly mammoth: A large, hairy prehistoric mammal that lived in the colder regions of the northern hemisphere.

For Further Exploration

Thomas G. Aylesworth, *Southern New England: Connecticut, Massachusetts, and Rhode Island.* New York: Chelsea House, 1988. A fact-filled volume about southern New England, highlighted with many black-and-white and color illustrations.

Amy Gelman, *Connecticut.* Minneapolis: Lerner, 1991. Fairly easy reading. Heavily illustrated with attractive color photographs.

Deborah Kent, *Connecticut.* Chicago: Childrens Press, 1989. Excellent color photographs, middle-grade reading level. Includes a timeline and a listing of important Connecticut citizens, past and present.

Lisa Sita, *Indians of the Northeast: Traditions, History, Legends, and Life.* Milwaukee, WI: Gareth Stevens, 2000. A trove of historical and cultural facts about the daily lives and cultures of Native Americans of northeastern North America. Attractively illustrated.

Arthur E. Soderlind, *Colonial Connecticut.* New York: Thomas Nelson, 1976. A middle-grade vocabulary, this volume covers Connecticut's history from its first explorers in the early 1600s to the approval of a federal constitution in the late 1780s. Black-and-white photos and illustrations.

Index

Algonquian
    life of, 8–10, 12
    tribes comprising lan-
        guage group, 7–8
    villages of, 10–12
Arnold, Benedict, 35

birchbark, 9
Block, Adriaen, 13–15
border, 4

canoes, 8, 9
children
    Algonquian, 12
    European, 20
Christianity, 29
Coastal Lowlands, 5
Colonial Wars, 31
Colt, Samuel, 36
Connecticut Valley
    Lowland, 4
constitution, 26–27

Declaration of
    Independence, 33–34

diet
    of Algonquian, 9
    of Paleo-Indians, 7
dugouts, 8
Dutch West India
    Company, 15

Eastern New England
    Upland, 4–5
economy, 36
England
    exploration by, 15–16
    French and Indian
        Wars and, 31
    Revolutionary War
        and, 32–35
    settlements by, 16–19
exploration
    by Dutch, 13–15
    by English, 15–16
    reasons for, 13

farming
    by Algonquian, 9
    currently, 4–5

by settlers, 19–20
food
  of Algonquian, 9
  of Paleo-Indians, 7
France, 31
French and Indian Wars,
  31
Fundamental Orders of
  1639, 26–27
furs, 12

government, 26–27
Great Britain
  exploration by, 15–16
  French and Indian
    Wars and, 31
  Revolutionary War
    and, 32–35
  settlements by, 16–19

Hale, Nathan, 34–35
Holmes, William,
  16–17
homes, 10
Hooker, Thomas, 18–19,
  26–27
House of Hope, 15
hunting, 6–7

Ice Age, 5–6

Indians
  early settlers and, 21
  French and Indian
    Wars and, 31
  land and, 15, 16, 21, 29
  warfare between set-
    tlers and, 22–25, 28,
    30–31
  see also Algonquian;
    Paleo-Indians

King George's War, 31
King Philip's War, 30–31
King William's War, 31

manufacturing, 36
Mason, John, 23, 24
Massasoit
  (Wampanoag), 29
Matabesec, 7
Metacomet
  (Wampanoag sachem),
  28–31
Mohegan, 8, 23–24

Narragansett, 23, 30
Native Americans
  early settlers and, 21
  French and Indian
    Wars and, 31

land and, 15, 16, 21, 29
population of, 12
warfare between
  settlers and, 22–25,
  28, 30–31
see also Algonquian;
  Paleo-Indians
Netherlands
  English settlers and, 17
  exploration by, 13–15
  Native Americans and,
  21
Nipmuck, 7

Oldham, John, 16–17, 23
Onrust, 14

Paleo-Indians, 6–7
Pequot, 7–8, 22–25
Pequot War, 22–25, 28
population
  Native Americans
  before Europeans,
  12
Puritans, 18–19

Queen Anne's War, 31

regions, 4–5

Sequin, 7
settlements
  by Dutch, 15
  by English, 16–19
slavery, 25, 31
Stamp Act, 32
statehood, 36
Stone, John, 23

Taconic Section, 5
Thurber, Charles, 36
Tiger, 13
trade
  Dutch and, 14, 15
  early, 12

universities, 37

van Curler, Jacob, 15

wampum, 9
Western New England
  Upland, 4
Whitney, Eli, 36
wigwams, 10
Winslow, Edward, 16
women, 9–11

Yale University, 37

Picture Credits

About the Author

Sheila Wyborny and her husband, a broadcast engineer, live in Houston, Texas. They enjoy flying their Cessna aircraft to interesting weekend locations and adding to their small antique collection. Mrs. Wyborny enjoys hearing from students who have read her books.